CUP AND SAUCER CHEMISTRY

Nathan Shalit

Illustrated by
Charles Waterhouse

DOVER PUBLICATIONS, INC.
New York

Copyright © 1972 by Nathan Shalit.
All rights reserved under Pan American and International Copyright
Conventions.

Published in Canada by General Publishing Company, Ltd., 30 Lesmill
Road, Don Mills, Toronto, Ontario.
Published in the United Kingdom by Constable and Company, Ltd., 10
Orange Street, London WC2H 7EG.

This Dover edition, first published in 1989, is a slightly abridged, slightly
corrected republication of the work originally published in 1972 by Grosset
& Dunlap, Inc., New York. Please note the addition of the warning on page
5. Some of the original illustrations have been deleted, and some have been
altered to depict the experiments more accurately.

Manufactured in the United States of America
Dover Publications, Inc.
31 East 2nd Street
Mineola, N.Y. 11501

Library of Congress Cataloging-in-Publication Data

Shalit, Nathan.
    Cup and saucer chemistry / Nathan Shalit ; illustrated by Charles
Waterhouse.
        p.   cm.
    "Slightly abridged, slightly corrected republication of the work
originally published in 1972 by Grosset & Dunlap, Inc., New York"—
T.p. verso.
    Summary: Simple experiments with materials available in the home
reveal basic chemistry principles.
    ISBN 0-486-25997-8
    1. Chemistry—Experiments—Juvenile literature. [1. Chemistry—
Experiments. 2. Experiments.] I. Waterhouse, Charles H., ill. II. Title.
QD38.S49 1989
542—dc19   89-1268
                                                                  CIP
                                                                  AC

A NOTE OF WARNING

CONTENTS

INTRODUCTION

You don't need a special chemistry set or expensive equipment to do many interesting and exciting experiments. Most of the things you need are probably right in your own home this very minute. This book will tell you how to do these experiments in your own kitchen.

Ask your parents if you have the following supplies in your kitchen or medicine cabinet: aspirin tablets, baking powder, baking soda (bicarbonate of soda), vinegar, clear ammonia, boric acid, rubbing alcohol, milk of magnesia, a candy or tablet laxative such as Ex-Lax, Feen-A-Mint, Alophen, or Espotabs. These, and others we will discuss, are easily available at your local drugstore or food market.

The equipment you need will be an empty dropper bottle or two (the kind nose drops come in); a few plastic straws; a teaspoon; a saucer; white paper towels; and some other things found in every home.

All the experiments described in this book will work if you follow the directions given. There may be other ways to get similar results. You may think of changes yourself. Try them.

None of the chemicals discussed is corrosive or will harm your skin.

Take special care when using ammonia. Follow directions. DO NOT smell or take a deep breath from the open bottle. The amount you smell while doing an experiment will not hurt you. If you get any on your skin, simply rinse or wipe it off.

Don't taste anything unless the experiment tells you to.

Before you begin an actual experiment, there are a few basic tools with which you should be familiar.

PIPETTE

A *pipette*, or small pipe, is a handy tool for transferring small quantities of liquid from one container to another. Instead of expensive glass pipettes, you will use ordinary plastic drinking straws. To use a pipette, hold it in your hand, as shown in the illustration, with the index finger above the top end. Dip the bottom end a half-inch or so into a liquid, press the finger down to close the top opening, and lift the straw out of the liquid. Now turn the straw slowly by moving your thumb and middle finger in opposite directions and the liquid will fall out of the bottom a drop at a time. Or, lift the index finger, and all of the liquid will fall at once. Practice with a glass of water. You will learn to do it in a minute or two. Never let the pipette touch a second liquid in an experiment. It should be held over the second liquid and dipped ONLY in the first. This will prevent your chemicals from getting mixed inside the pipette.

Rinse the pipettes well after each experiment so they will be clean and ready for later use.

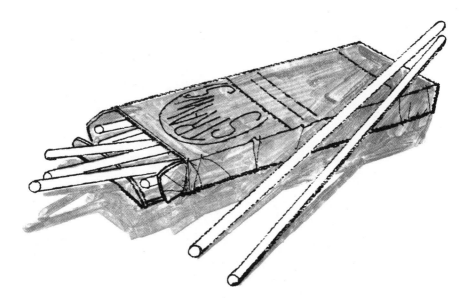

FILTER

To *filter* means to separate a liquid and a solid, like dirt and water, by passing the mixture through a filter paper. The solid is left behind when the liquid goes through the paper. This liquid is then called the filtrate. In the laboratory, special filter papers are used with a funnel. You will use paper towels, or filter papers used in brewing coffee, and a funnel, if you have one, or an ordinary small wire strainer.

To make a filter paper, place a cup or saucer upside-down on a sheet of paper towel and draw a circle around it with a pencil. Cut out the circle. Now fold it twice, as shown in the illustration. Next, open it in your hands so that there is one layer on one side and three layers on the other. You now have a paper cone that will fit snugly into a funnel, or loosely into a strainer.

To use the filter, place it into the funnel or strainer and carefully pour into it the mixture you want to separate. Mix up some sand, food particles, or loose dirt with water in a small juice glass. Messy, isn't it? Pour the mixture into your filter and collect the filtrate in another glass. If the filtrate doesn't come through clear the first time, pour it back into the same filter and let it go through a second time. The filtrate may become colored, like tea or mouthwash, but it is clear. You can see through it. It doesn't have anything floating around in it.

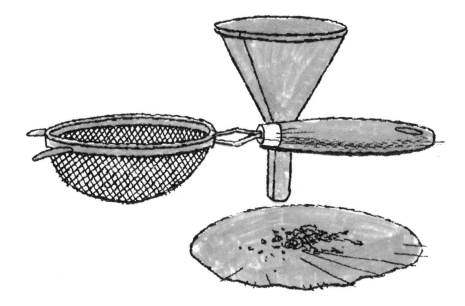

(An ordinary tea bag is really just a bunch of tea leaves sealed up in a filter paper. Water goes in and colored flavored water comes out, but the solid tea leaves stay inside.)

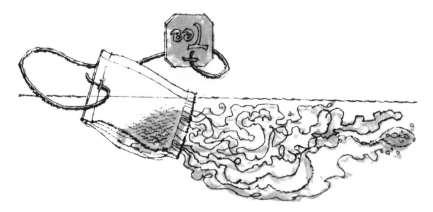

TEST TUBES

Whenever people think of experiments, they think of *test tubes*. But every experiment in this book can be performed without a test tube, and more easily, too. Instead of a test tube, you will use an ordinary saucer. Every saucer has a "well" in the center that is there to hold the cup. This well will be your working area. Use a saucer with a clear well that doesn't have any cracks or markings in it.

Now you must organize yourself. You should work in the kitchen when everything has been cleaned up after a meal. You will use the sink, and a small area alongside it. Some experiments will be done on a burner or two of the kitchen stove. Work in a small area and do only one series of experiments at a time. Throw away finished tests and clean up as you go along. Get a notebook and pencil to keep a record of your experiments. Write down what you used, what you did, and the results. All scientists keep such notebooks. Keep orderly records so you do not become confused and lose track of things. Be neat.

Any chemicals that are saved from one day to another must be clearly and correctly labeled. If you use second-hand bottles or jars, soak off old labels with warm water before you use them. Never leave a wrong label on a bottle. Never keep any chemical that is unlabeled.

By acquiring these good habits, you'll get more fun out of experimenting.

Before doing each experiment, read it through, so you'll be familiar with what is going on, and so you'll have all the things you need close at hand.

Now you are ready to do some real experiments that will show you some interesting things about chemicals.

ACIDS AND BASES

Chemicals can be divided into acids, and their opposites, bases. A base is frequently called an alkali. Acids taste sour. You can taste some orange, grapefruit or lemon juice. These contain citric acid. It is concentrated most in the lemon; therefore, the lemon is the most sour. Mix a small quantity of vinegar and water. Taste it. See how sour it is. It is called acetic (a-SEE-tic) acid.

Bases don't taste sour. They are sort of bitter. Taste a pinch of baking soda. Put your tongue on a wet bar of soap. Ecchh! These taste-tests are really simple experiments. Old-time soap-makers used to taste the soap mix to ascertain when the proportion of alkali in it was just right.

Here's a word you should know. When two or more chemicals are mixed and something happens, something new is formed. There has been a reaction (ree-ACK-shun). The chemicals have reacted.

SOLUTIONS AND SOLUBILITIES

This series of simple experiments will show you some more facts about chemicals which will be interesting and useful.

You will need several small jars or glasses; hot and cold water; alcohol (whenever alcohol is suggested in this book, 70% ethyl rubbing alcohol is meant); nail-polish remover; paint thinner (which is also called mineral spirits or charcoal starter fluid); dry-cleaning fluid or spot remover; and mineral oil, baby oil or salad oil. Do these experiments on a Formica or old wooden surface, since alcohol and nail-polish remover can harm some furniture finishes and painted surfaces.

When a solid substance is mixed with a liquid, and the solid seems to disappear, it is said to have gone into solution. The molecules of the solid have spread among the molecules of the liquid. This liquid is called the solvent. The substance that went into solution is called the solute. If a substance will dissolve in a liquid, it is said to be soluble in that solvent. If not, like sand, it is said to be insoluble. Solids are soluble to varying degrees in different solvents. They are said to be very soluble, slightly soluble, or insoluble. Two liquids which are soluble in each other, like alcohol and water, are said to be miscible. Temperature influences solubility; generally, heat hastens solution and increases solubility.

All this information about specific chemicals and other substances is of importance to chemists, candy-makers, cooks, farmers, and laundries. It enables them to use their chemicals to best advantage.

You will see in experiments on page 70 how a chemical can be changed so that it becomes soluble or insoluble. Here are some solubility experiments that are different, since there are no chemical changes. Only simple solutions are demonstrated.

1. Prepare two glasses of water—one with cold water from the faucet, and one with very hot water. Into the hot water put a spoonful of sugar and stir. See how it quickly dissolves with only two or three stirs. Now put a spoonful into the cold water. See how much longer it takes to go into solution.

Put a spoonful of sugar into a quarter of a glass of alcohol. Stir. Does it go into solution? Not as easily as in water. Try a bit of sugar in nail-polish remover, cleaning fluid, paint thinner. Record your results. Wash these glasses thoroughly with warm water and detergent when you are finished.

2. Hang a tea bag over each of two glasses. Into one put cold water. Into the other, boiling water. The ingredients of the tea dissolve better in one than the other. Try a tea bag in a small glass of alcohol, then paint thinner.

3. Cut a small pile of chips from a candle. Put some in jars of (a) water, (b) paint thinner, (c) nail-polish remover, (d) alcohol. Cover each with a lid of aluminum foil and allow to stand for a day or so, swishing them around once in a while. In which is the wax soluble?

4. Do the same experiment, using half-teaspoonfuls of salad oil instead of candle wax. Compare your results.

5. On separate sheets of clean white paper, draw a line with a ball-point pen. On each put, separately, a few drops of water, alcohol, paint thinner, nail-polish remover, and mineral oil. In which of these solvents is the ink most soluble? Such knowledge can be useful if you want to remove an ink mark from clothing.

6. Do the same experiment as in No. 5, using a crayon instead of ball-point ink. Compare the results. How do the results of this experiment compare with No. 3?

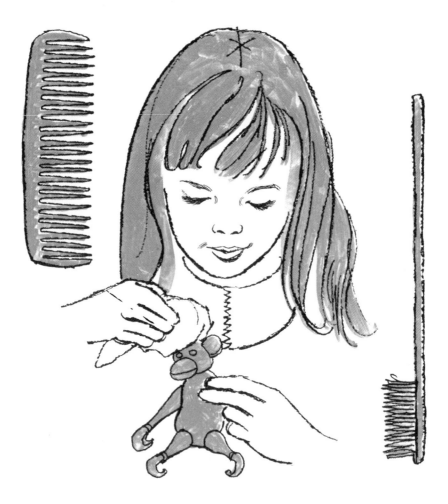

7. Prepare an old plastic comb, a toothbrush handle, a plastic pill vial, a piece of old painted tin or wood (like an old toy), and a snip of acetate rayon cloth (ask your mother). You know without even trying them that none of these is soluble in water, but what would be the result in some of your other solvents?

Get several pieces of clean dust rag. Moisten a corner with one of the solvents and rub one of the items collected. Is there any change in the surface? Has the shine or paint been removed? If so, it means that the item is soluble in the solvent. Try all of the solvents on each of the items. Most of these items are soluble to some degree in acetone, the chief ingredient in nail-polish remover.

8. Shave a teaspoonful of chips from a bar of soap. Put half in some water and half in some alcohol. Cover them and allow to stand for several hours. In which is the soap more soluble? Is it ever completely soluble? To test whether any soap went into solution, pour some of the clear liquid into an empty glass and pour water into it. Do you get suds?

SOLUTIONS, WITH COLOR-CHANGE

You will need several small jars with tight-fitting lids; some tincture of iodine; and several oils, like salad oil, mineral oil, baby oil and mineral spirits (paint thinner). Before you do this experiment read the first three paragraphs on page 52.

On page 81 are some experiments with oil and water. Oil and water do not mix; they are immiscible. This experiment involves two immiscible solvents.

Fill each of four jars about half-full of water. Into each carefully put about five drops of iodine. (Work on <u>thickly</u> folded newspapers, in case you spill any iodine.) Pour the iodine carefully, as shown on page 52. Shake. Each jar is now about half-full of light-brown iodine solution.

Into separate jars, pour a little of the mineral oil, salad oil, baby oil and mineral spirits. Close each jar tightly, and shake vigorously for a minute. Set them all aside to settle for two or three minutes.

See what has happened. Since the iodine is more soluble in the oils than in water, it has been transferred from the water solution to the oil solution. Iodine in oil solution is purple, which is the true color of iodine. The brown color of the tincture of iodine is due to a loose chemical combination of iodine and potassium iodide. Since the salad oil is a vegetable oil, it acts somewhat differently. Here the solution is still brown. If you allow it to stand for several days, it will slowly lose the brown color. The iodine slowly combines chemically with the oil, and apparently disappears.

SOLUTIONS AND SPECIFIC GRAVITY

When you dissolve a substance in a solvent, the resulting solution is heavier than the solvent alone. It is said to have a greater specific gravity.

Salt water is heavier than plain water. Syrup is heavier than water. Heavy things tend to sink, lighter ones to rise.

You can demonstrate this in many ways. Here are two.

Fill a tall, clear glass with boiling water and allow it to stand for a minute or so. Now carefully hang a tea bag over the edge of the glass so that it is submerged in the hot water. Look at it closely. The water is dissolving something out of the tea leaves. Since this solution is heavier than the water, you can see the brown solution streaming from the tea bag to the bottom of the glass.

Snip a top corner off a tea bag and spill out the dry tea leaves. Put a spoonful of sugar in the bag. You now have a "sugar bag." Hang this over the edge of a glass of water. Hold a sheet of white paper behind the glass and look closely. You can see the sugar solution streaming out of the bag, just as with the tea solution.

Pure water is said to have a specific gravity of one. Iron has a specific gravity of nine; it is nine times as heavy as water. It sinks. Oil has a specific gravity of 9/10. It is lighter than water. It floats.

Heat expands things and they then become relatively lighter. Hot water is lighter than cold water. When you boil a pan of water, the water at the bottom becomes hot and rises first. Colder water takes its place at the bottom, whereupon it, too, gets heated and rises. The process goes on, round and round, until all of the water has been heated and it boils.

You can demonstrate this movement. Here's how.

Fill a saucepan half-full of water and add a few shakes of pepper. Stir it well so that the pepper sinks to the bottom. Put it on the stove with a small flame. The pepper granules will swirl around as they are carried by the heated water.

PHENOLPHTHALEIN T.S.

Now it's time for some "real" experiments. You will need: a saucer, a teaspoon, rubbing alcohol, laxative candy or pill (Ex-Lax, Feen-A-Mint, Alophen or Espotab), a dropper bottle, a bar of soap and various items from the kitchen. Any laxative pill will do if it has phenolphthalein in it. Read the label to find out. Pronounce the name out loud: feen-ole-THAY-leen. The middle "ph" is silent.

Fill the dropper bottle with rubbing alcohol and pour it into the saucer. Put the pill into the saucer and crush it with the back of the teaspoon. Crush it as fine as you can, and mix it well with the alcohol. Let it settle for a moment. Then transfer this alcohol solution of phenolphthalein into the dropper bottle. Use your dropper to do it. The dropper is really a pipette with a rubber nipple. You now have a bottle of phenolphthalein test solution. Label it: PHENOLPHTHALEIN T.S. (The T.S. means Test Solution.) Chemists call this an indicator. It indicates or shows something. This solution indicates the presence of alkalis or bases by turning pink.

See how it works.

Swish a bar of soap in a cup of water. Add a drop of phenolphthalein T.S. It turns bright pink. This indicates that soap has an alkali in it. Soap is made by boiling a mixture of fats or oils and a strong alkali.

Now explore the house for things to test with your **T.S.** Bring **them to** the kitchen sink and make each test in a clean saucer. Wash the **saucer** thoroughly after each test and rinse it well. This will prevent one **test** from affecting another. Try your indicator on ordinary detergent, baking soda, washing soda, vinegar, milk of magnesia, dishwasher detergent, washing-machine detergent, powder cleanser, toothpaste, shaving cream, sugar, ammonia and permanent-wave solution. Some of these are alkaline and some are not. Compile a list.

Take a piece of eggshell and crush it very fine in your saucer with a half-teaspoonful of water to get a very fine wet powder. Add a drop of indicator. A very faint pink color should result. Eggshell is a very weak base or alkali. We will discuss it again later.

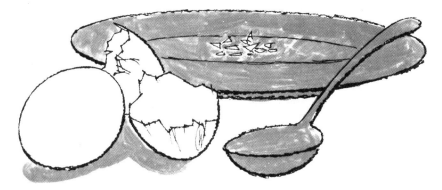

MORE INDICATORS

The next time you go to a market, buy a head of red cabbage. It is a beautiful vegetable, dark purple in color. Cut up a piece so that you have about a cupful of chopped leaves. Fill the cup with boiling water and allow it to stand for about five minutes. Pour off the resulting purple liquid into a glass or jar. If you save any from day to day, keep it in the refrigerator in a jar labeled cabbage water.

Cut strips about an inch wide and several inches long from a white paper towel. Dip several of these into the cabbage solution and set them aside to dry.

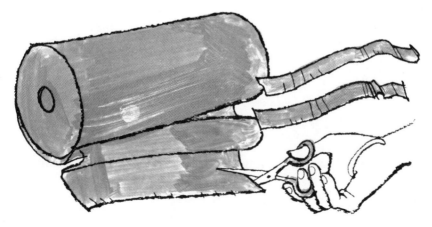

In separate glasses, make solutions of several of the bases you handled in the last experiment: soap, baking soda, washing soda and ammonia. Put a few drops of each of these on separate strips of your cabbage paper. See the change in color. Put a few drops of vinegar or lemon juice on the changed spot. See it change back to the original color.

Pour some of your cabbage water into a soup bowl or a clear glass. Add one of your alkaline solutions and see a beautiful color-change.

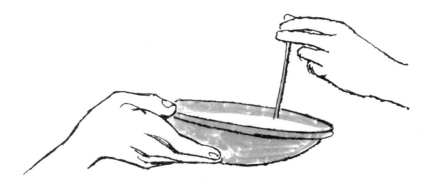

The coloring matter in various vegetables is sensitive to acid-base changes. Try similar experiments with beet juice, spinach or any colored vegetable or fruit juice.

TURMERIC

On your mother's spice shelf you may find a can of powdered turmeric or curry powder (which contains turmeric). If not, get a can from your local market.

Put a teaspoonful or so into a small glass or jar and add a quarter of a glass or less of rubbing alcohol. Allow it to stand for a few minutes.

Make strips of turmeric paper the same way you made the cabbage paper. Repeat the experiments with turmeric that were performed with the cabbage solution or the phenolphthalein test solution.

These make very colorful solutions. Try large jars or bowls filled with solutions of these indicators, about a spoonful to a quart of water.

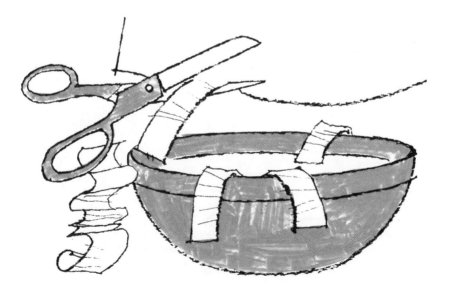

SECRET WRITING

Secret writing is done with an ink which is invisible until treated in some way to bring out the words. Four kinds are discussed below.

You will need, for all of them, a clean penpoint (nib) and penholder. This is the kind that was used before the invention of the ball-point pen. Ask your parents if they have any. If not, you must go to a stationery store to get a set. If you get a brand-new point, hold it in the flame of a match for a second to burn off the oil. This will allow the point to retain the ink. When you have finished using the pen, wash and dry the point before you put it away.

1. Lemon juice. Write your message, using lemon juice as ink. When dry, it will be invisible. To make it visible, the paper must be heated over a flame. Be careful not to get the paper too hot or it will burn. If you are careful, the message will appear as if written with brown ink.

2. Milk. Use this just like the lemon juice.

3. Phenolphthalein. Make a solution as described on page 28, using Feen-A-Mint. When dry, it will be invisible. To develop the writing, the paper may be dipped in soapy water or water that has a little ammonia added to it. You can also see the writing if you sponge the paper with a paper towel wet with the water-ammonia mixture. The writing will appear in pink. When the ammonia evaporates, the writing will disappear again.

4. A secret ink can be made by stirring a spoonful of starch in a glass of boiling water. This ink, when dry, will also be invisible.

To bring it out, prepare a soup bowl with five or ten drops of iodine and a half-cup of water. Dip the sheet in this. Many papers have starch in them, so the whole sheet may turn blue, but the writing will appear much darker than the paper.

ASHES AND MORE ASHES

You will need phenolphthalein T.S., a paper towel, a funnel or strainer, a saucer, cigarette ashes, fireplace ashes or charcoal ashes. Get an ashtray before your mother empties it. Throw away the matches and cigarette ends, leaving only the ashes. Put a tablespoon-

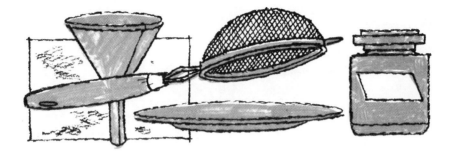

ful or so of water into the ashtray and mix it for about half a minute. Filter this mess and collect the filtrate on a saucer. Test it with your phenolphthalein T.S. What happens? What was in the ashes? Repeat the experiment with other types of ashes. What are the results? All plant products, when burned, leave an ash that contains potassium carbonate. Potassium carbonate is an alkali.

This experiment can also be done without the filter arrangement. With a pipette, transfer a small amount of the water-and-ash mixture to a sheet of paper towel. The ashes will stay where you dropped them, but the liquid will spread out on the paper. Now put a drop of the T.S. at the edge of the wetted paper, and watch the pretty pink ring form.

The early settlers in this country made their soap by soaking their fireplace ashes in water and cooking this solution with fats saved in the kitchen. Some people still make their own soap, but they buy their alkali under the name of "lye."

Following are three more chemical words you ought to know. Pronounce each one out loud so that you will know what it should sound like. Then when you and other chemists discuss your experiments, you will understand each other.

Reagent: pronounced ree-AGE-ent. A reagent is any chemical used for testing.

Effervesce: pronounced eff-er-VESS. It means to produce bubbles, to fizz, like Coca-Cola, or Alka-Seltzer.

Carbonate: pronounced CAR-bone-ate. A carbonate is a chemical that has the gas carbon dioxide locked up in it. Carbonates are all weak alkalis. Remember the eggshell experiment?

CARBONATES AND ACIDS

You will need a juice glass or cup, pipette, teaspoon, baking soda or washing soda, vinegar.

The acids you find around the house are acetic acid (vinegar) and citric acid (fruit juices: orange, lemon or grapefruit). These react with carbonates to release the carbon dioxide; they effervesce. Remember this rule: all carbonates effervesce in the presence of acid. So if you have some carbonate T.S., you can hunt for acids.

To make carbonate T.S., put a teaspoonful or so of baking soda or washing soda in a cup half-filled with water. Stir a few times, and allow it to settle. The clear liquid is your T.S.

Pour a small quantity of vinegar in a saucer. With your pipette add a little T.S. What happened? Rinse the saucer and repeat with the following: orange juice, grapefruit juice, tomato juice, apple juice, coffee and tea. Try various flavors of bottled soda. First, however, stir them vigorously to remove the carbon dioxide put in by the manufacturer to make them fizz. Which of all of these contain acid? List them.

MORE CARBONATES AND ACIDS

You will need vinegar, a pipette, a saucer, eggshell, clamshell, oyster shell, marble chips, an empty medicine bottle, a balloon and sodium bicarbonate tablets or Tums. You may be able to get the seashells from a market where fresh fish is sold. Marble chips may be obtained from a pet store or a hardware store that sells them for driveways. A drugstore can supply the sodium bicarbonate (or soda-mint) tablets or Tums.

In separate glasses put each of the following: a piece of eggshell; a piece of clamshell, oyster shell or pieces of any sea shells; marble chip; sodium bicarbonate tablet. Pour enough vinegar into each to cover the piece. Wait for a minute or two and observe the reaction closely. See all the tiny bubbles forming on the surface of the shell? These are bubbles of carbon dioxide. All the shells, Tums and marble are made of the same chemical: calcium carbonate.

Try this experiment with a piece of chalk. (Chalk is made up of the tiny, tiny shells of billions of minute sea animals that lived many millions of years ago.)

Get a clean medicine bottle, such as the kind that holds cough syrup, and fill it more than half-full of vinegar. Drop in a half-dozen tablets of sodium bicarbonate or two or three Tums. Stretch a balloon over the top, as shown in the illustration. Watch. As the carbon dioxide is formed, it fills the balloon, which is soon upright.

Baking soda, or sodium bicarbonate, decomposes in water and changes into sodium carbonate, or washing soda. This latter is a stronger base than the baking soda.

Here's how to demonstrate this.

Put a pint or two of water into a measuring pitcher and stir in a tablespoonful of baking soda. Add a few drops of phenolphthalein test solution. You should have a nice pink solution. Put half a glassful of this solution aside as your standard. Put the rest into a saucepan and boil it. After it has boiled for a minute, pour out half a glassful to compare with your standard. Continue to boil the rest for a few minutes. Then pour this into a glass and compare with the first two glasses. The solutions in the second and third glasses are of a deeper red color because they contain a greater proportion of sodium carbonate.

CANDLES AND CO₂

The chemical formula for carbon dioxide is CO_2. It is a gas formed by the burning of carbon or the destruction of a carbonate by an acid, as discussed on page 39. CO_2 is an invisible gas and is heavier than air. It will not burn. In fact, it will smother a fire by depriving the fire of a supply of oxygen (air). Most fire extinguishers depend on this principle to put out fires.

To see this, put several teaspoonfuls of baking soda in a large jar. Set up a lighted candle close by. Pour a little vinegar into the jar. When the effervescence quiets down, add some more vinegar. This effervescence produces CO_2 and drives the air out of the jar. Hold a lighted match close to the mouth of the jar. The flame will go out.

Carefully lift the bottle and pour the CO_2 out of it just as if you were pouring water. You can't see the CO_2, but it is there. Pour the CO_2 over the candle flame. As if by magic, the flame will go out.

Carbon is one of the things that make up all living things, from microbes to elephants to trees. As long as animals or plants are alive, they use carbon in one way or another to build their bodies. In the body process called metabolism, they produce heat by burning carbon and forming carbon dioxide. When you exhale, part of your breath is carbon dioxide. When you burn wood, gasoline or coal, one of the things you form is carbon dioxide. You come in contact with these carbon dioxide processes every day. The "holes" in your bread or cake are created by carbon dioxide. You can demonstrate this easily.

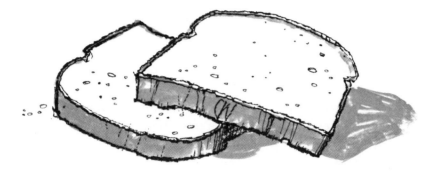

In making bread, flour is mixed with water and yeast and set aside. Yeast is a living plant that consumes some of the flour and produces carbon dioxide (CO_2). The bubbles of CO_2 push through the dough and form the holes.

Sugar and flour are chemical cousins, so we can use sugar in this experiment.

You will need a clear ketchup or soda bottle, some yeast, sugar and a toy balloon.

45

Into a glass of warm water mix a few spoonfuls of sugar and a small bit of yeast. Pour half of this mixture into the bottle, and set it aside for a few minutes. While you are waiting, inflate the balloon to full size and hold it that way for a minute — this will stretch and soften the rubber. Let the air out, and then put the balloon on the bottle so that it makes a tight fit. Set this arrangement aside for an hour.

Set aside the partly-filled glass of water-sugar-yeast mixture, too, where it won't be disturbed by movements of air.

After an hour you will see a good evolution of bubbles, filling and erecting the balloon. Changes will also have taken place in the glass.

Flour, sugar, starch, and honey are examples of a class of substances called carbohydrates. These are all used as food. They can all be acted upon by yeast, as you have seen. This process is called fermentation.

In its life process, the yeast, while producing carbon dioxide, also produces alcohol. This is the basis of the production of all wine, beer and whiskey.

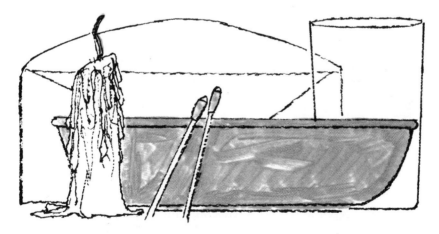

CANDLE CHEMISTRY

You will need a short candle, a glass tumbler, a soup bowl, matches and a scrap of white paper.

In order for a candle to burn, the wax must first be melted and then changed into a gas. This is done when the hot flame of a match is touched to the wick. The wick is needed to concentrate the melted wax into one place. The heat of the flame then continues to melt more wax, changing it into a gas for burning. The wax-gas right next to the wick is not burning. It only burns when it moves to the outside of the flame where it can get oxygen from the air.

You can prove this easily with a scrap of stiff white paper. An old white envelope will work fine. Do this experiment next to the sink, so that if the paper starts to burn you'll have a safe place to drop it. Hold the piece of paper in the flame for a few seconds, down close to the wick, as shown in the illustration. Do not hold it there long enough to catch fire. Slide it in, hold it a few seconds, take it out. You should have a burned ring with a clear center. If it doesn't work the first time, try again, leaving the paper in a bit longer.

CANDLE GAS

Another way to prove that there really is a gas being formed at the wick is as follows. Light the candle and allow it to burn for a minute or so to develop a small pool of melted wax at the base of the wick. Hold a lighted match in one hand. Blow out the candle and immediately bring the burning match close to the wick, but not touching it. As the match approaches the wick, the candle will burst into flame.

Repeat several times. As the match approaches the smoking wick, from above or from the side, the gas will ignite, as if by magic.

Take a piece of aluminum foil about an inch and a half wide and a few inches long. Wrap it around a pencil to make a short tube. Leave a little bit to twist into a handle.

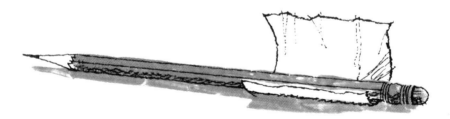

Now, hold this tube in one hand, close to the flame, and a lighted match in the other. Blow out the candle flame, holding the tube close to and over the wick. Bring the burning match toward the top of the tube. A flame will flash through the tube and ignite the candle.

MORE WITH A CANDLE FLAME

The previous experiment showed that a candle flame is made of burning gas. It has other things in it, too. Candle wax is basically a compound called a hydrocarbon, similar to gasoline or fuel oil. It is composed of hydrogen and carbon, both of which can burn. The heat of the flame decomposes (breaks up) the compound and then burns the carbon and hydrogen. When carbon burns, it forms carbon dioxide. When hydrogen burns, it forms water.

Some of the carbon in the flame does not burn. But these tiny pieces of carbon get very hot and glow. This is what makes the flame visible and produces light.

You can see the carbon and the water.

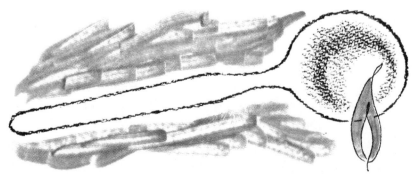

Hold a cold, dry spoon or white saucer in the flame of the candle for just a few seconds. Look at it. You will see beads of moisture and black soot on the spoon. This is the water and carbon from the flame.

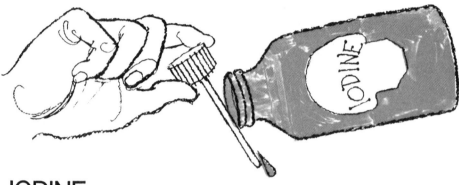

IODINE

You will need a bottle of tincture of iodine, a clean plate and several items of food from the kitchen.

When handling iodine, be careful not to spill any. It will stain almost anything it touches, and is sometimes very difficult to remove. Work over the sink or on a thick layer of newspaper or an old magazine.

When pouring tincture of iodine from its little bottle, hold the rod which is attached to the inside of the cap as shown in the illustration. The iodine will then run down the rod and go exactly where you want it.

Transfer a little of the iodine to a clean dropper bottle, and add an equal quantity of water. Label this IODINE T.S.

Iodine is a specific test for starch. Iodine turns starch blue. If you put iodine on something and the something turns blue, it has starch in it. Starch is one of the basic foods we eat. It is a carbohydrate, and is made by many plants. Test several vegetables. Put a drop of T.S. on a slice of potato, sweet potato, lima bean. Try prepared foods or cereals like bread, spaghetti, bacon, corn, cereal. Some of these have starch, some do not.

Starch is used to stiffen clothing before ironing. Test by putting some iodine T.S. on a corner of the tail of a white shirt. To remove the dark blue mark, rub it with a bar of wet soap until it is decolorized. The soap is a base, and iodine forms a new compound with a base.

IRON

Iron is a very useful metal with which you can do several interesting experiments. For our purpose, the best form of iron around the house is steel wool. Since steel is almost all iron, you can use it as if its name were "iron wool." If the steel wool in your house has soap in it, the soap must be completely washed out of it or it will spoil the experiments. To do this, hold the pad under running warm water, pulling it slightly apart and turning it until all the soap is gone. Let it dry. You can buy plain steel wool in any hardware or paint store. It comes in many grades of fineness. One of the finer grades is better than the coarsest grade.

IRON OXIDE: Two Experiments

You will need two clean steel wool pads, pliers or tweezers or ice tongs, chlorine bleach solution, hydrogen peroxide (hereafter referred to as "peroxide") from the drug counter, glasses, a saucer, a quart jar, a candle and matches.

Iron rusts in wet air. That is, it combines with oxygen; it burns. To demonstrate this, take a piece of clean steel wool, wet it, pull it apart so that it is somewhat looser and fluffier than when new. Stuff this into the bottom of a tall glass. Turn the glass with the steel wool up-side-down in a saucer and fill the saucer with water. Put this aside for a day or two. Watch what happens. The iron will react with the oxygen in the air in the glass and become rusty. As the oxygen combines with the iron, water will enter the glass to take its place. Water will rise in the glass.

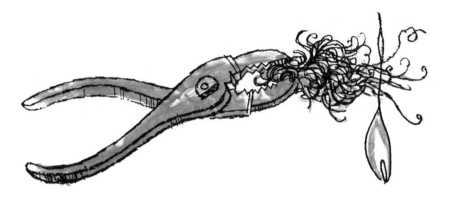

Using the pliers, hold a piece of clean steel wool in a gas or candle flame. It gets white-hot and burns. Let it cool. Rub it between your fingers. It crumbles. It has turned to rust. It is iron oxide.

To do the next experiment, everything must be prepared and ready. Line up the materials you will need: steel wool, pliers, candle, an empty jar about one quart size, peroxide and bleach. Light the candle. Pour about an inch of peroxide into the jar. Add about the same amount of bleach. The mixture will effervesce and bubble up, vigorously producing oxygen. Hold the steel wool with the pliers in the flame of the candle for a moment to get it burning. It will look like little red bugs running up the wires. Then hold the steel wool in the jar.

What happens? You should have gotten a bright shower of white sparks in the glass.

The chlorine released pure oxygen from the peroxide, and the iron burned rapidly in the oxygen. This experiment is best done next to the sink. Be **very careful** with the chlorine bleach. If any spills on your clothing it will leave a bleached spot!

IRON TANNATE

You will need a saucepan, a tea bag, steel wool (old and rusty is good —but no soap, remember?), vinegar, filter and peroxide.

Certain iron salts form a black color with tannic acid. This was the basis of old-fashioned permanent inks. The following two experiments take somewhat longer than the others, and ought to be enough for an evening's work.

Put a tea bag into a cup and fill the cup about a quarter-full of boiling water. Let it soak five minutes. Throw away the tea bag and set the solution aside. Label it TEA.

Take a piece of steel wool—one of the rusty ones from the previous experiment is fine. Put it into a saucepan (aluminum, enamel, steel, or glass—it doesn't matter) and cover it with vinegar. Bring it to a boil and let it simmer for about five minutes. Transfer this mess to a filter and collect the filtrate in a juice glass. The filtrate should be almost colorless. Add a few drops of hydrogen peroxide. The solution should turn a bright reddish brown. You have combined the iron with the acetic acid and the peroxide to form ferric acetate solution. Put this aside and label it FERRIC ACETATE.

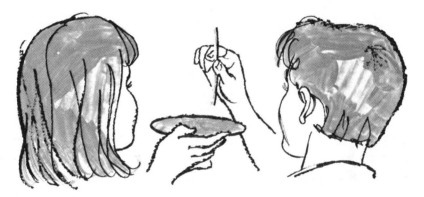

Now, with a pipette, put a few drops of the iron solution into a saucer, and with a different pipette add a few drops of tea. You should get a dark black color immediately. You have formed ferric tannate.

The Latin word for iron is *ferrum,* so chemists refer to iron compounds as either ferrous or ferric.

You can taste the ferric acetate solution. It puckers your mouth; it is astringent. Iron is a useful tonic for some people who need it to build up their blood.

FERRIC HYDROXIDE

Make a new solution of iron and vinegar. (Do NOT add peroxide at this point.) Pour a little of the solution into a saucer. Add a small amount of ammonia. A greenish deposit of ferrous hydroxide has been formed. Now add a few drops of peroxide. It now changes to a rich red color. This is ferric hydroxide.

To the rest of the solution of iron in vinegar, add a few drops of peroxide to form the brown solution. Pour some of this into a saucer and add ammonia. Again you have formed the red ferric hydroxide.

IRON: More Experiments

You will need ferric acetate solution, raisins and cream of tartar baking powder.

Ferric iron plus tartaric acid forms a green color.

Dissolve about a quarter of a teaspoonful of cream of tartar baking powder in a little water. Allow the effervescence to slow down. Pour some of this solution into your saucer. Add ferric acetate solution. Swish it around. You should see a greenish color.

Get a dozen or so raisins and chop them up. Put them into a cup and cover them with warm water. Squash them and push them around with your fingers. All raisins contain sugar and cream of tartar. Pour into a saucer some of the solution you have just made. Add a bit of ferric acetate solution. Swish it around. You should detect the greenish color you saw with the baking powder.

Raisins are only dried grapes. Grapes are used to make wine. In making wine, cream of tartar is left in the wine casks. All the cream of tartar and tartaric acid used in candy-making comes from these wine casks.

OXYGEN AND AIR

Air is about 20%, or one-fifth, oxygen. Now, if you have a glassful of air, and take out the oxygen, something else must go into the glass to take up the space.

This was demonstrated by the experiment on page 54, where the iron combined with all the oxygen in the glass.

This can be demonstrated more rapidly with a candle.

Stand a candle, about half the length of the glass, in a dry saucer. Do this by melting the bottom a bit with the flame of a match. Fill the saucer about half full with water. Light the candle. Put the glass upside-down over the candle. The candle will burn until it uses up all of the oxygen, and then will go out. Water will rise in the glass to take the place of the oxygen.

ASPIRIN

You will need four or five aspirin tablets, ferric acetate solution, a filter, alcohol, a saucepan and iodine T.S.

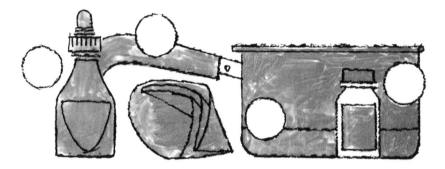

Aspirin is an interesting chemical made from salicylic (sal-i-SYL-ik) acid and acetic acid. Chemically it is usually called acetyl salicylic acid. But if you want to impress your friends, you can call it "mono acetic acid ester of salicylic acid."

The tablet is made in a machine that squeezes the aspirin powder together with another substance into the familiar round shape. What is this other substance? Break a tablet in half. Test one half with iodine T.S. Is there starch in the tablet? Test the other half with the ferric acetate T.S. If the tablet is fresh, nothing should happen in this second test.

Now, put three or four tablets into a saucepan and add enough water to cover them. Boil until most of the water is gone. Do not let it get completely dry or it will burn and spoil the experiment. Let the pan cool for a few minutes. Aspirin is a weak chemical that can be easily broken up into its original parts, acetic acid and salicylic acid. This is what you have just done. Pour some alcohol, about one-fourth of a cup, into the saucepan and swish it around for a while. Pour everything into a filter. Collect the filtrate in a juice glass. Test the white stuff left in the filter with iodine T.S. On a saucer test a few drops of the filtrate with the iron T.S. Iron forms a dark blue color with salicylic acid. We cannot test for the acetic acid because it was lost in the boiling, and there is no easy test for the beginning experimenter.

COLOR FLAME TESTS

You will need boric acid, salt, cream of tartar baking powder, a wire coat hanger, copper-cleaner powder and assorted coins.

Metals burn with different-colored flames. This kind of test helps chemists identify chemicals. It is the most important way astronomers have to tell what the sun and other stars are made of.

Fashion a piece of wire, as shown in the illustration, from a coat hanger. Hold the end in the gas flame until all of the paint burns off. Let it cool. Now put a little boric acid in the small loop, and hold it in the flame. The flame burns with a green color.

Many households do not have a gas-burning kitchen stove. To do these experiments that require a flame, you will need an alcohol burner. You can make one very easily using a clean mustard jar or a baby food jar with a metal cap. Buy a kerosene lamp wick at a hardware store. Poke a hole in the jar's lid with a screwdriver so that you have a narrow hole into which the wick will fit snugly. Poke the hole from the inside of the lid. For fuel buy a container of methanol fuel such as Dry-Gas (or any other brand of the same substance). This is available at auto supply stores and supermarkets. The back of the label must say, "This contains METHANOL." If it says "isopropyl alcohol" or any other chemical, it is not suitable. Ask your parents to help you.

The next experiment must be done over the sink.

To a quarter of a glass of alcohol, add a quarter teaspoon of boric acid and stir well. Allow the excess boric acid to settle to the bottom. Take a spoonful of this alcohol solution and hold it over the sink. Have someone else light a match and touch it to the spoonful

of solution. It will burn with a beautiful green flame. Try it at night with the kitchen lights out. Isn't it pretty! Be careful. If you spill any of this, you will be spilling fire! I repeat: work over the sink, so that if you spill any, you can rinse it away with water.

Pick up some ordinary table salt in your wire loop and hold it in the gas flame. The bright yellow flames show that sodium is burning. The chemical name for salt is sodium chloride.

Sodium is a metal. Another metal similar to sodium is called potassium. Cream of tartar is made with potassium. If you hold some of this powder in the flame, it will burn with tiny violet sparks. If it doesn't work at first, sprinkle some of the powder into the flame. You will then be sure to see the violet sparks. This is a test for potassium.

Get some Cameo brand copper-cleaner powder, the kind that comes in a shaker can. Sprinkle a **tiny bit** on a wet penny. Make a tiny bit of very wet paste on the penny. Place the penny over a gas burner as shown in the illustration. (You must first prepare the wires by burning off all the paint.) Turn on the flame. In less than a minute the flame will turn to a beautiful green. This is a test for copper. Repeat this experiment with the other coins: a nickel, a dime, a quarter. If you can find some, try the old silver coins, as well as the new sandwich kind. Did you know that all U.S. coins now contain copper?

NEUTRALIZATION

Early in the book we discussed acids and bases. Here is another experiment along this line.

When an acid is mixed with a base they neutralize (NEW-tral-eyes) each other and form a "salt." Ordinary table salt, called sodium chloride, is one kind of salt. You can make a different salt. Here's how.

Mix one-fourth of a teaspoonful of milk of magnesia (a base) with a spoonful or so of water in a saucer. Add a drop of phenolphthalein T.S. Now add lemon juice (citric acid), a few drops at a time. Stir after each addition. Continue until the milky pink liquid turns clear, like water, and the pink color disappears. At this point the magnesium hydroxide (milk of magnesia) has been neutralized by the citric acid to form magnesium citrate. If you do the experiment with vinegar instead of lemon juice, magnesium acetate will result. If you warm this solution or put it aside in a saucer until all the water evaporates, you will be left with small crystals of the salt.

PRECIPITATES

This is another good chemical word: precipitate (pree-SIP-i-tate). As a verb, it means to fall out. As a noun, it means the stuff which has fallen out. Earlier in the book we described an experiment where you formed iron tannate. The iron tannate precipitated out of solution. Iron tannate is a dark blue precipitate. The weatherman uses the word when he refers to rain or snow. He may say, "Precipitation is expected this afternoon." The water will precipitate out of the air. It will rain or snow.

You can do another experiment to produce a precipitate.

You will need epsom salt, clear ammonia and a glass.

To one-fourth of a glass of water add a few tablespoonfuls of epsom salt (magnesium sulfate). Stir it well until it is all dissolved. Now fill the glass with ammonia. Stir. The white precipitate is magnesium hydroxide or milk of magnesia. Allow it to settle.

Pour off some of the clear liquid from the top, and set it aside in a saucer for a few days until all the water evaporates. You will be left with crystals of ammonium sulfate.

ANOTHER PRECIPITATE

A small container of alum can be purchased at any drugstore. Your mother may have some in the medicine cabinet, or she may have used some to make pickles.

Dissolve a teaspoonful of alum in a fourth of a glass of water. Slowly add ammonia, and stir. A thick white precipitate will form—this is aluminum hydroxide. Add vinegar. The white precipitate will dissolve and you will have a clear solution of aluminum acetate.

Aluminum hydroxide will also precipitate from an alum solution if you add a solution of washing soda or baking soda. Any base will do it.

If you have added a drop or two of phenolphthalein T.S., you can watch the pink color come and go as you change from an alkaline to an acidic solution.

CRYSTALS

You will need sugar, one tall glass, a short length of white string, a pencil and a clean metal weight, like a paper clip or washer or nut.

Bring a glassful or more of water to a boil. Fill a tall glass right to the brim with sugar. Slowly pour boiling water into this glass. As the sugar gets wet, it will sink. Dig a spoon or fork into the sugar right to the bottom of the glass to wet all the sugar. Add the boiling water until the glass is almost, but not completely, full. Stir for a few minutes to dissolve the sugar.

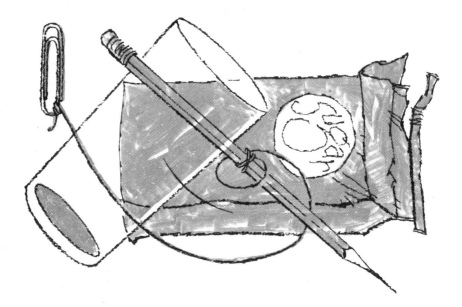

Tie a small weight to one end of a piece of clean white string, and roll the other end of the string around the pencil as shown. The string should be just about long enough so the weight will almost touch the bottom of the glass. Drop the string into the glass. Set the arrangement aside uncovered in a warm place where it won't be disturbed for several days. Watch the crystals grow on the string. You are making rock candy, or sugar crystals. Crystals will also grow on the inside of the glass and will form a crust on the surface. Break up this crust so that water can evaporate. As more water evaporates, more crystals will grow.

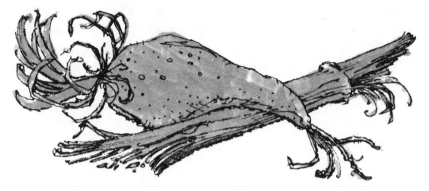

Sugar is made from the juice of the sugar cane or the sugar beet by a similar process. The juice is warmed to evaporate the water and allowed to crystalize. Crystals are a very pure form of a chemical. Making crystals, called crystallization, is an important way of purifying chemicals.

You can do a similar experiment with ordinary table salt.

When you buy table salt, you are buying a million tiny crystals of sodium chloride. But because they are so small and have been knocked around in processing and handling, you cannot see, even with a magnifying glass, the true beauty of the individual crystals.

Every chemical forms its own type and shape of crystals. Those of salt are cubes—perfect little squares.

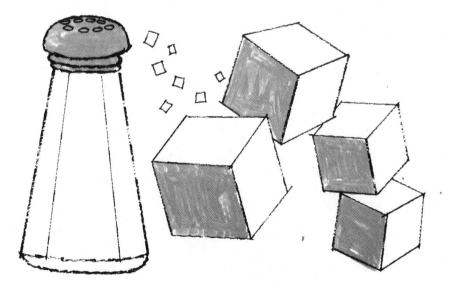

To see these, fill two glasses half-full of salt. Add water to almost fill both glasses and stir well for a few minutes. Allow the excess salt to settle to the bottom of the glasses. Each glass now contains a saturated solution of salt. The solution will not be clear at this point because table salt is not pure sodium chloride. Tiny amounts of other chemicals are added to help keep it dry; however, this will not affect the experiment.

Saturated means that the water has taken up all the salt it can hold. If some of the water is lost due to evaporation, some of the salt must go out of solution as crystals. This is what will happen in this experiment, just as with the sugar experiment.

Prepare a string just as you did in the previous experiment. Do this in one glass. Keep the second glass covered with a piece of aluminum foil. Use this as a reservoir of salt solution.

As the glass with the string loses water and crystals form on the string, add more salt solution from the reservoir. Watch the crystals grow. With the two-glass arrangement you can keep the experiment going for several weeks, and the salt crystals will grow quite large. You will will have clusters of beautiful cubical crystals.

They will be large enough to be seen and appreciated without the use of a magnifying glass.

STILL MORE CRYSTALS

Crystals can also be formed by cooling a melted or vaporized solid without the use of a solution. Diamonds and other mineral crystals were formed by such a process.

For this experiment you will need a double boiler, some ice cubes, and some paradichlorobenzene crystals. (Pronounce it slowly: para-di-klor-o-ben-zeen.) These are the para crystals your mother uses when she puts winter woolens away for the summer. It is obtainable in any drugstore or market.

In the top (smaller) part of the double boiler put a tablespoonful or two of para crystals. Fill the bottom (larger) part of the double boiler with cold water and a handful of ice cubes.

Now put these together in reverse of the usual way, as shown in the illustration—the small part with the para on bottom, and the large part with the ice water on top as a lid. Put this on the stove on very low heat and leave for a few minutes (two or three ought to do). Now carefully lift the top part and look at its bottom. It should be covered with a blanket of small needle crystals of para. Allow the lower section to cool and you will see that its bottom, inside, is covered with a solid crystalline layer.

Both these pots can be cleaned with hot water and a soap-steel wool pad.

The next experiment is set up exactly the same way as the previous one. But instead of para, use moth balls or moth flakes. These are a different chemical, called naphthalein. Pronounce it: naf-tha-leen.

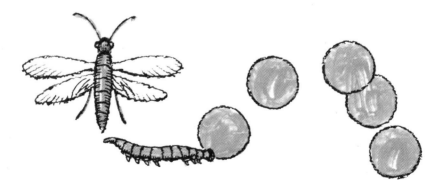

You will find the bottom of the upper pot covered with light, thin, flaky crystals, like snow.

To clean up after this experiment, pour the melted naphthalein from the lower pot into an old tin can and discard with the trash. DO NOT pour it into the sink. DO NOT burn it. Wipe the two pots well with paper towels. Then they should be thoroughly washed and scoured with a steel wool soap pad or scouring powder and then hot water and detergent.

This series of experiments shows several different types of crystals. All chemicals in their pure state will form crystals of a distinctive shape. Examination of crystals by X-ray and other means help chemists to identify unknown substances.

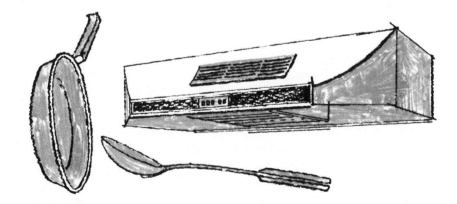

CARAMEL

You will need sugar, a frying pan, a wooden spoon or other long handled spoon, and an exhaust fan over the stove.

Root beer, Coke, and most manufactured or processed foods that are brown contain caramel color. This is sugar that has been heated until it turned brown, but was not allowed to burn. You can make some in the kitchen, if there is an exhaust fan over the stove.

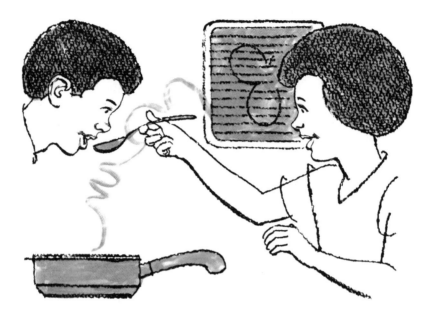

Put a few tablespoonfuls into a dry frying pan. Turn on the heat. Stir slowly as the sugar starts to melt. Turn the heat down a bit and continue to stir as all the sugar melts. Continue to heat and stir until all the white sugar has disappeared. Turn the heat down low. The brown liquid will start to boil. Stir. It will become quite a dark brown. Turn off the heat. You now have caramel. It is dark brown. You have caramelized the sugar. It is VERY HOT at this point, much hotter than boiling water. LET IT COOL OFF. Add some water and then taste it. There is no longer any sweet taste. See the nice brown color.

You can clean up after this experiment by merely soaking the pan and utensils in water for ten minutes. Everything will dissolve and rinse off easily.

CHARCOAL AND FLAMES

On page 44 you learned that all living things are made of carbon (and other things). Charcoal is the carbon that is left when wood is destroyed in a certain way. This experiment will show you how to make charcoal.

A flame is a burning gas. You saw this in the experiment with the candle flame.

When wood burns, there is a flame because the heat decomposes it and gas is formed. Both the carbon and gas burn. But if wood is heated so that it can't get any air, it will be destroyed in a different way. Several new things will be formed. Gases will be formed. This experiment will show what happens.

IMPORTANT. This experiment should be done only if you have an exhaust fan over the kitchen stove that exhausts to the outdoors.

For this experiment you will need two tin cans, a glass of ice water, and a few small pieces of wood or a handful of sawdust or wood chips available from any lumber yard or butcher (who uses sawdust to sprinkle on his cutting-room floor).

Prepare two cans that fit together loosely. A tuna fish can and a soup can are fine. The tuna fish can will act as the lid for the other can. (See illustration.) Punch a hole in the lid can with a large nail or an ice pick. Make the hole large enough to accommodate a pencil. The hole should be off to one side, not in the center. Remove all labels and glue from the cans.

Put a handful of sawdust or several small pieces of wood into the lower can and cover with the lid. Place this arrangement on the stove and turn on the burner. Turn on the exhaust fan.

In a few minutes you will see smoke coming out of the vent hole. Hold a lighted match to this smoke. At first the smoke will be composed of too much air and moisture, and the match will go out. But after a while the smoke will burn with a steady flame. This smoke contains the gases of the chemically destroyed wood. The process going on in the can is called destructive distillation. Tars and gases are being formed. But no matter how hot the wood gets, it can't burn because no air can get to it.

Set a glass of cold water on the lid so that the gases coming out of the vent go up around it. Add an ice cube now and then. Moisture will form around the glass. So will some dark gooey stuff—tar. Continue the heating for thirty minutes or more. Turn off the heat and allow the arrangement to cool thoroughly before you try to handle it. While waiting, you can wash the glass well with cleanser powder to remove the tarry smell.

Now examine your cans. The inside of the lid has black tar on it. The bottom can has charcoal in it. Examine it on a sheet of clean paper. Put a piece of the charcoal on a burner to get it burning. It burns with a steady red glow, but no flame. The gas-forming part of the wood is all gone. In the chemical industry the gases and tars are used to manufacture many different chemicals.

EMULSIONS

Have you ever heard someone say that oil and water don't mix? This may be true to a certain extent, but there are many ways to make them mix. When oil and water are well-mixed, you have an emulsion (ee-MULL-shun). They are mixed by means of an emulsifying agent. The following experiments will illustrate this. First you must get yourself four or five small jars with tight-fitting lids. Jars about the size of baby food jars are perfect.

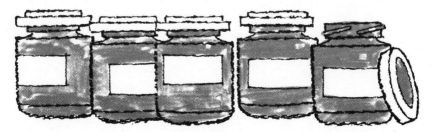

Fill each jar one-third full of salad oil, and one-third full of water. Close the first and shake well. What happens? The oil separates into small balls called globules. But when you let the jar stand a minute or two, the oil and water separate again. So, oil and water don't mix. But, into the second jar add a bit of detergent. Now shake hard, very hard. The oil and water are more evenly mixed and form a sort of creamy mixture. The oil is broken up into very small globules and stays that way. If you had mixed this up in an electric mixer, you would have a really smooth creamy mixture. Into the third jar, put an egg yolk. (Ask your mother to show you how to separate the yolk from the white of the egg.) Shake very hard again. Again, you have a good emulsion. Into the fourth jar add some mucilage—the clear amber kind that comes in a glass jar with a slit rubber spreader. Shake well again. Once again, you have an emulsion. The mucilage contains gum arabic, which is widely used as an emulsifying agent. The egg yolk contains cholesterol (kole-ESS-ter-ole). Your body makes cholesterol to help use the fats that you eat. Mayonnaise is an emulsion made of vinegar, salad oil and eggs. One of the ways soap and detergent clean things is by emulsifying the fats and oils that hold the dirt.

CATALYSTS

Sometimes a chemical reaction won't take place, or will proceed very slowly unless some other substance is added. This other substance, the catalyst (CAT-a-list), hastens the reaction but does not itself take part in the reaction. Catalysts are widely used in the chemical industry to speed up reactions. An important use of catalysts is in the making of gasoline from crude oil.

You can demonstrate a catalytic reaction. Get a few lumps of sugar and a bit of tobacco or wood ashes. Hold a lighted match to a corner of the cube of sugar. It may melt and get black, but it won't burn. Now rub a tiny bit of the ash on the sugar, and hold a flame to it. It immediately starts to burn and will continue to burn.

The ash had a catalytic action. It helped start the oxidation of the sugar.

COPPER

You will need some pennies, a glass and ammonia.

Copper is a very interesting metal. One of its uses is to harden silver. You saw in the experiments on page 67 that our silver coins contain copper. Unless your house is very, very new, all the electric wire is made of copper. (Many new houses have aluminum wire.)

This first experiment is very simple. Just put four or five old pennies in a glass and add one-fourth of a glass of ammonia. Put the glass aside and look at it a few hours later. The ammonia is turning slightly blue. Leave it for several days. Each day, you can add ammonia to replace the amount which has evaporated. Your solution will be turning a darker and darker blue. It is a beautiful blue color. Leave it for four or five days altogether. This blue solution will be used in the next experiment. It is called copper-ammonium complex.

REDUCING SUGARS

You will need the copper solution made in the last experiment, a saucepan, two or three saucers, washing soda, pipettes, a teaspoon, and one or more of the following: honey, jam, a grape or raisin, orange juice, sweet corn, milk.

The sugars contained in honey and many fruits are different from table sugar. They are called simple sugars. One is dextrose, or grape sugar. These sugars will react with the blue copper solution and form a red precipitate. Chemists say the copper has been reduced. This experiment will demonstrate this reaction.

Put a small amount of water in the saucepan and bring it to a boil. Turn down the heat so it just simmers, and cover the pot with a saucer. While the water is heating, add a half teaspoonful of *washing soda* (not baking soda) to a small glass of the blue copper solution, and stir. Label this ALKALINE COPPER SOLUTION. With a pipette, transfer some of this solution to the saucer well. Now, to the solution in the saucer add a speck of honey no bigger than a grain of rice. Watch it for a minute or so. The blue solution will gradually turn reddish. If you stir it with a toothpick, the entire blue disc will turn red.

Remove the saucer (careful, it's hot!) and wash it well. Repeat the experiment with the grape, a drop or two of orange juice, and the other things. Wash the saucers well before using for food.

This reaction is a very important one in medicine. People who have diabetes use a similar copper solution or paper test strip to test their urine to see if it contains sugar.

COPPER PLATING

You will need vinegar, two small glasses, ten or fifteen dull pennies and a big nail.

Put ten or fifteen dull pennies into a small glass and pour in enough vinegar to cover them. Sprinkle in a few good shakes of table salt. Swish the glass around.

The action of the salt and the vinegar cleans up the pennies. It dissolves the surface corrosion and leaves the pennies bright.

This solution now contains salt, vinegar and some copper.

Take a good-sized iron nail, and first clean it thoroughly with steel wool and soap, or powdered cleanser. Rinse it off. Put it into the solution you have just made. If the solution in the glass is not deep enough to cover an inch or so of the nail, wrap the nail in a very small piece of paper towel before you put it into the solution. This will act as a wick and carry the solution to the nail.

Look at the nail after five or ten minutes. It is covered with a bright coat of copper.

What has happened is that some of the iron went into solution and caused the copper to come out of solution.

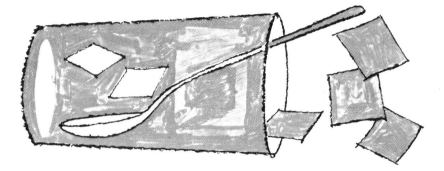

HYDROGEN

You will need a tall glass, or jar, aluminum foil, washing soda and hot water.

Hydrogen is the simplest and lightest of all elements. It is so light that the earth's gravity cannot hold it, and any loose hydrogen escapes into space. Hydrogen is probably the original building block of all the elements found on earth or anywhere in space. It burns; that is, it combines with oxygen to form water.

You can make hydrogen easily. You can see it forming and you can burn it. Here's how.

Prepare a dozen or so small flat pieces of aluminum foil, about the size of a postage stamp. Drop them all into a tall glass or jar. Add a few tablespoonfuls of washing soda. Fill the glass almost full with very hot water from the faucet. Stir well. Cover the glass with a piece of aluminum foil, and smooth down all around the edge to form a snug-fitting lid. Make a small hole in the center of this lid with a ball-point pen.

Look closely at the mixture. You will see many tiny bubbles forming all over the pieces of aluminum foil. This is hydrogen. In fact, there are so many bubbles, they lift the pieces to the top. Since hydrogen is lighter than air, it accumulates above the surface of the liquid and escapes through the small hole. After the reaction has been going on for two or three minutes, hold a lighted match close to the hole. You should be rewarded with a distinct *pop*. Smooth down the aluminum-foil lid and wait another two minutes. Try again. *Pop* again. You are producing miniature explosions. If you are lucky, instead of a *pop*, you may get a steady flame.

Now remove the cover from the glass and add a squirt of detergent. Poke the whole mixture with a spoon or fork and allow some bubbles to form. Put a lighted match to the bubbles. You should hear tiny little *pop-pop-pops*.

SOAP

In the experiment with cigarette ashes we mentioned that soap could be made with the alkali found in wood ashes. You can do it now. Here's how.

In a saucepan made of stainless steel, glass or enamel, but NOT aluminum, put a juice glass full of salad oil, or used kitchen fats like bacon grease or fat skimmed from gravy. Add an equal amount of water and an equal amount of washing soda. Bring the whole mess to a boil. Reduce the heat, so that it doesn't splatter. Swish it around occasionally or stir it with a stick. After a while, as the water boils away, you will see a change in consistency, and you no longer have just oil and water. Simmer it for five or ten minutes and then take it off the heat. Allow it to cool. You now have a pan of soap.

Take a spoonful out and put it in a jar. Add hot water, and shake. You should have nice rich suds.

This is the basic method of manufacturing soap. However, do not try to wash with your soap. Because of the lack of good chemical control, your soap may be too harsh, or it may be too greasy.

WATER—HARD AND SOFT

This experiment may take a few days of preparation. One of the things you need is a soap solution. You can buy this in a drugstore as tincture of green soap, or you can make your own. You cannot use a shampoo or household detergent, since these are mostly chemical detergents and not really soap.

To make your own soap solution, cut up half a cupful of soap chips from a bar of soap. Transfer to a jar and cover it with alcohol. Allow this to soak for a day or so. The alcohol will dissolve enough soap for these experiments. Put the solution into a dropper bottle and label it STANDARD SOAP SOLUTION.

You must have four or more clear medicine bottles of the same size, or small jars with tight-fitting lids.

You must collect several different samples of water. Put these into your bottles so they are about half-full. Collect: tap water (cold water from the faucet); tap water that has been boiled; melted clean snow or melted frost from the freezer of your home refrigerator; rain water; water from a friend's house in a different town; water from a stream, pond, ocean. In fact, collect as many different "kinds" of water as you can think of. You can "manufacture" some water: add a pinch of Epsom salt to one jar of tap water and a pinch of plaster of paris to another. Put a label on each jar so you will know exactly what you have.

These various samples are not chemically pure water; they may contain one or more minerals in tiny amounts. This depends on where they came from. Water with minerals in it is called hard water. Water with little or no minerals in it is called soft water. Minerals in water combine chemically with soap so that the soap cannot clean. Soap and water will lather only after all the minerals in the water have combined with soap. That is why hard water wastes soap and does not clean as well as soft water.

You can gauge how hard water is by seeing how much soap is needed to produce good suds. Here's how.

Line up your jars, each filled with an equal quantity of water. Label each jar as to the source of the water. Prepare a chart, as illustrated. Work with one jar at a time. Into a jar add one drop of soap solution. Always keep the dropper in the same vertical position so that the drops will always be the same size. Cap the jar and shake vigorously. Allow to stand. Do you have rich suds? If not, add another drop of soap solution. Shake, and look again. Each time you add a drop, make a mark on your chart. Keep on adding one drop at a time until you have good permanent suds.

When your experiment is over, you will have a line of jars, each with water and suds. Your chart will indicate the number of drops of soap solution you put into each jar. Thus you will be able to compare and note the hardness of the various samples of water.